Home of the Deer, the Fox and the Beastly Squirrels

The Warren
Home of the Shy Rabbits

Hollow
Tree

Squirrel Wood

Steep Hill

Cliffs

Steep Hill

More Cliffs

Steep Hill

The Utterly Otterleys

Pa

Ma

Otto

Ottina

Crab Cove
Farm

Cliffs

Crab Cove

Driftwood Bay

To Sam and Ewan
THE UTTERLY OTTERLEYS by Mairi Hedderwick

First published in 2006 by Hodder Children's Books

Text and illustrations copyright © Mairi Hedderwick 2006

Hodder Children's Books
338 Euston Road, London NW1 3BH

Hodder Children's Books Australia
Hachette Children's Books, Level 17/207,
Kent Street, Sydney, NSW 2000

A catalogue record of this book is available from the British Library.

ISBN: 9780340873694

10 9 8 7 6 5 4 3 2

Printed in China

Hodder Children's Books is a division of Hachette Children's Books.

The Utterly Otterleys

Mairi Hedderwick

Hodder
Children's
Books

A division of Hachette Children's Books

THE UTTERLY OTTERLEY family lived in a cosy burrow, which Pa Utterly Otterley had carefully dug out of the warm, brown earth. A door of neatly woven willow and ferns led inside to a comfy couch with cushions of sea pinks. Seaweed curtains framed a large window overlooking the bay which was full of mackerel. Their home was perfect.

One morning, however, Pa Utterly Otterley woke in a bad mood.

'I didn't get a wink of sleep!' he grumped. 'The door kept banging and the moonlight came through the curtains.'

'The door could be stopped, dear, and the curtains made thicker,' suggested Ma.

'No,' announced Pa Utterly Otterley. 'I'm finding us a new home.'

Ma was quite taken aback. Otto and Ottina were upset.

But Pa always knew best, so they packed the pots and pans and toys and trailed out the door after him. All day long, Pa Utterly Otterley loped inland following the river.

'Can't we have a rest?' implored Ma, after a while, weary of her load.

'We're hungry,' mewed Otto and Ottina. But Pa led on.

'HERE IT IS!' beamed Pa Utterly Otterley.

The family squeezed through a tiny opening into a dark

cave. 'Perfect,' he said. 'No window, no door! I'll find

some food.'

Ma got a fire going. Otto and Ottina played ghosts but when it was time to go to bed, they missed the sea pink cushions and their tummies were rumbling, for Pa had only found a handful of worms.

'I'll catch a big trout tomorrow,' he promised.
'Sleep well.'

But nobody slept well.

The wind whistled through the tiny entrance and in the darkness, no one knew when it was morning.

'We're moving,' grumped Pa Utterly Otterley.

'HERE IT IS!' beamed Pa Utterly Otterley.

Behind a high waterfall was another cave. Ma, Otto and

Ottina flung themselves down on the thick carpet of moss.

'Perfect,' said Pa. 'A stained glass window and door in one.

And this is where the salmon leap.'

Hungrily, the Utterly Otterleys waited for salmon to leap.

None came.

'Whatever,' said Pa. 'We'll sleep well tonight.'

But nobody slept well.

Heavy rain flooded the waterfall into the cave.

Soaking wet and starving hungry, Ma and the children
followed Pa over a moor.

The rabbits disappeared deep into their cosy burrows when they saw them coming. Just like our own dear home, thought Ma. 'Couldn't we stay here?' she suggested. 'No!' grumped Pa Utterly Otterley. 'Follow me!'

'HERE IT IS!' beamed Pa Utterly Otterley. 'Dry as can be!'

Shelves of mushrooms and nuts lined the inside of

a hollowed out tree.

Hopefully, Ma unpacked her pots and pans.

Otto and Ottina somersaulted in the bed of rustling leaves,
laughing and squeaking.

The mushroom and nut stew didn't taste too bad, but Otto
and Ottina asked, 'Can we have mackerel tomorrow?'

'No,' said Pa Utterly Otterley. 'No sea. We eat what we find.
Sleep well.'

But nobody slept well.

They woke to a terrible screeching. Nuts rained down on them.

'Go away! This is *our* home!' the squirrels screamed.

'We want *our* home,' wailed Otto and Ottina.

'Please, Pa,' beseeched Ma. 'There was nothing wrong with our old home.'

'No,' grumped Pa Utterly Otterley. 'Follow me!'

'For the very last time,' muttered Ma, somewhat
belligerently, as she shouldered her battered
pots and pans.

Although they were going downhill, it was hard plodding through the snow, so the Utterly Otterleys tucked their tails up onto their tummies and slid down on their bottoms.

'I smell the sea!' sniffed Otto.

'I smell mackerel!' sniffed Ottina.

'HERE IT IS!' beamed Pa Utterly Otterley, opening a door
of neatly woven willow and ferns almost hidden by a snowdrift.

'This is *quite* the most beautiful home I have ever seen,'
smiled Ma. 'Isn't Pa clever to find us such
a perfect home at last?'

'Oh, yes!' chorused Otto and Ottina.

Delighted, Ma carried in her pots and pans.

'I'll light the stove, my dear,' said Pa helpfully.

Then Pa said: 'I know exactly where to go for mackerel for supper, which is rather strange, don't you think, this being our new home?'

Ma, Otto and Ottina smiled at each other but didn't answer.
They knew that everyone would have a good feed and a good
night's sleep and that Pa Utterly Otterley would never ever
talk about moving home *ever* again.

Home of the Deer, the Fox and the Beastly Squirrels

Hollow Tree

The Warren

Home of the Shy Rabbits

Squirrel Wood

Steep Hill

Cliffs

More Cliffs

Otto, Ottina and Wee Pet Crab make a Snow Pa

Steep Hill

The Big Slide

Steep Hill

Crab Cove Farm

Cliffs

Crab Cove

Driftwood Bay

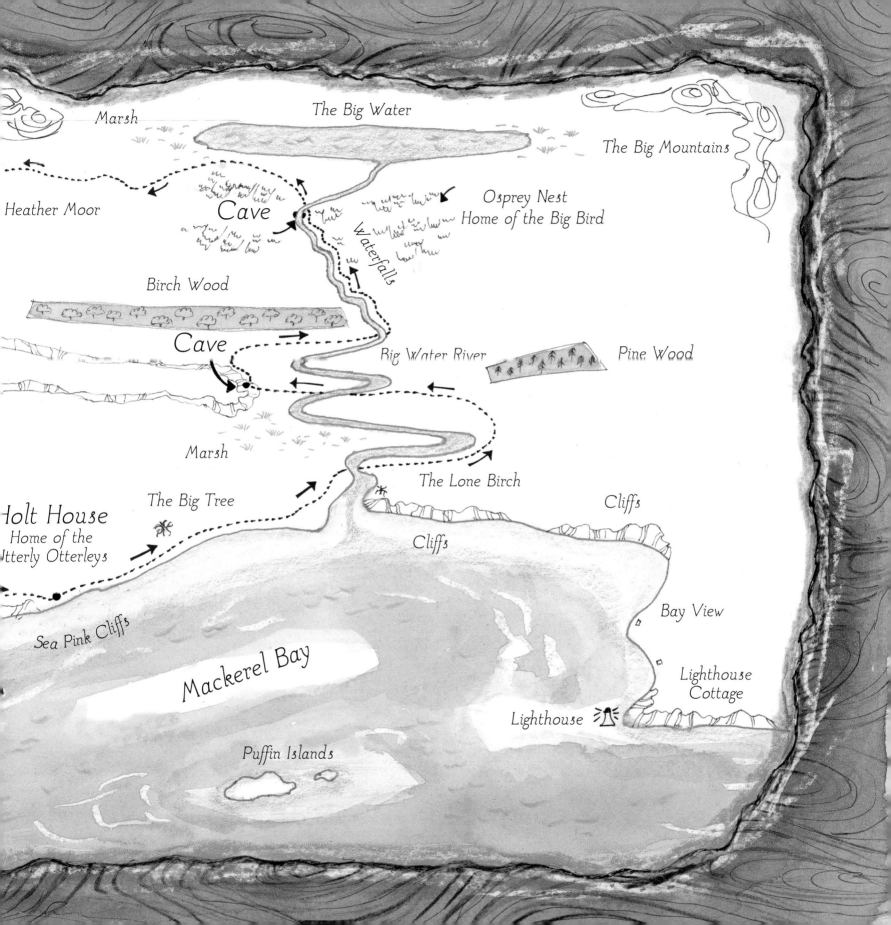